The Dance Of Words

Stepping to the Beat of Meaning

Chirag Pandya

India | USA | UK

Made with ❤ on the BookLeaf Publishing Platform
www.bookleafpub.in
www.bookleafpub.com

Dedication

To the **Tribhuvan Guru and the Eternal Gardener** *in whose sacred garden I'm but a flower, blooming only by His love and compassion.*

Preface

Words are powerful—they build bridges, open doors, and bring the world closer together. For students learning English as a second language, words can feel like a mountain to climb. But once conquered, this mountain reveals a breathtaking view of limitless opportunities and connections.

This collection of poems is a heartfelt effort to help students discover the magic of words and the joy of vocabulary. Designed for learners at every stage—from preschoolers learning their first rhymes to higher secondary students expanding their linguistic horizons—these poems aim to break the barriers of hesitation and instill confidence in speaking and understanding English.

For young learners, the playful rhythm and engaging themes will make their first steps in language fun and memorable. For older students, the deeper insights and vibrant imagery will awaken their curiosity and passion for expression. At every level, these poems are crafted to spark creativity, foster learning, and encourage a love for English.

Teachers will also find these poems a valuable resource to engage their students. By blending education with creativity, they can make language learning an enjoyable and enriching experience. These poems offer a way to inspire students to embrace words, fall in love with language, and realize that English is not a subject to fear, but a world to explore.

It is my hope that this book will serve as a stepping stone for every student who feels uncertain about learning English. Let these poems remind you that with words, you hold the key to unlocking your potential and shaping your dreams.

Welcome to a world where words come alive—step in and let the magic begin!

Chirag Pandya

Acknowledgements

This book would not have been possible without the support of the BookLeaf Publishing and the encouragement of many wonderful people who believed in the vision behind this work.

First and foremost, I extend my heartfelt gratitude to all the students who inspired this journey. Your curiosity, struggles, and triumphs in learning English as a second language motivated me to create something meaningful to support your growth.

To the teachers who dedicate themselves to nurturing young minds, thank you for being a guiding light for your students. Your passion for education and your belief in the power of words are the true catalysts for change.

I am deeply grateful to my mentors and colleagues who provided invaluable feedback, encouragement, and insights throughout the creation of this book. Your wisdom and guidance have been instrumental in shaping this collection.

A special thank you to my family and friends, whose unwavering support gave me the strength to turn this dream into reality. Your belief in me has been my greatest source of inspiration.

Finally, I thank every reader who picks up this book. Whether you are a student, a teacher, or a lover of words, I hope these poems ignite your passion for language and show you the transformative power of words.

This book is a labor of love, and I dedicate it to everyone who dares to dream, learn, and grow through the magic of language.

Chirag Pandya
https://www.fb.com/Chirag0810

1. Dance with Words

Life's a stage, a scripted play,
Yet unscripted truths light the way.
We chase the stars to find our place,
But starry dreams can leave no trace.

Together we rise, but to get there we fall,
A giant leap often starts so small.
The past may haunt, the present may heal,
Yet presence of mind sharpens the deal.

Heartfelt words can open a gate,
But a hardened heart seals its fate.
Time ticks slow when you're standing still,
Yet fleeting moments can time distill.

Silence speaks, but it never tells,
Lies may echo where truth dwells.
Freedom calls, but free doom waits,
The choice is yours, decide your fates.

Love's a climb, but it pulls you down,
The higher the hopes, the harder you drown.
Broken trust can build a wall,
But walls crumble when forgiveness calls.

The light we seek is inside, not far,
Yet we search outside, chasing the star.
Darkness stays till dawn departs,
For night's end is where day starts.

So dance with words, let meanings twist,
Let paradoxes fill your list.
For life is clever, a riddle untold,
Where plays with words are worth more than gold.

2. The Joy of Words

Words are happy, words are bright,
They make our world full of light!
"Jump" up high, "down" we go,
"Fast" we run, then "slow" we flow.

"Clap" your hands, "stomp" your feet,
"Spin" around, feel the beat!
"Smile" so big, "laugh" out loud,
"Wave" your hands, feel so proud!

"Hello" is warm, "goodbye" is sweet,
"Please" and "thank you" are so neat.
"Big" is tall, "little" is small,
"Happy" words for one and all!

Words are fun, words are kind,
They help us learn and feel so fine.
So talk and play, and sing today,
With words, we laugh and shout hooray!

Words are colors, bright and new,
They paint the sky, and flowers too!
"Run" and "stop," let's play the game,
"Jump" and "sit," it's all the same!

"Look" around, "find" a friend,
"Clap" your hands, the fun won't end!
"Up" is high, "down" is low,
"Round" we go, watch us glow!

"Big" is large, "small" is neat,
"Fast" and "slow," feel the beat!
"Hello" we say, "bye-bye" we wave,
"Yes" we cheer, "no" we behave!

Words are magic, words are play,
They help us learn and laugh all day!
Sing them loud, say them bright,
Words bring joy and pure delight!

Words are stars, twinkling bright,
They make our world so full of light!
"Jump" and "hop," let's dance around,
"Twirl" and "skip," let's make a sound!

"Big" is wide, "small" is fun,
"Up" we go, "down" we run!
"Look" and "see," let's find some joy,
"Wave" to the sun, and play with a toy!

"Happy" we are, "sad" we're not,
"Slow" we go, "fast" we trot!
"One" and "two," we learn to count,
"Sing" a song, and laugh a mount!

Words are magic, words are grand,
They help us learn and understand!
Speak them kindly, share their grace,
Words bring smiles to every place!

Words can giggle, words can play,
They can chase the clouds away.
With a "hello" and a "how are you,"
Words can make a friend or two.

"Up" goes high, and "down" is low,
"Fast" can run, while "slow" can go.
Words like "bright" can bring the sun,
And "funny" words can make life fun!

"Big" is tall, and "small" is tiny,
"Sweet" like honey, "sour" like lime-y.
"Happy" words bring smiles to faces,
"Sad" ones take us to quiet places.

So use your words with love and care,
They're magic that you can always share.
Speak them softly, or let them sing,
Words, my friend, can do anything!

Words are tiny, words are tall,
Words can build or break a wall.
They tell a story, sing a song,
They help us know where we belong.

"Quick" is fast, and "slow" is steady,
"Wait" says stop, "go" means ready!
"Bright" like sunshine, "dark" like night,
Words can paint the world in light.

With "please" and "thanks," we show we're kind,
With "sorry," peace is easy to find.
Words like "brave" can make us strong,
Words like "help" can right a wrong.

They bring us laughter, wipe our tears,
And fill our hearts with joyful cheers.
So choose your words with love and care,
For they have magic to share everywhere!

Words are strong, like mighty trees,
They flow like rivers, dance like bees.
With just a word, you can inspire,
Or light the world like a glowing fire.

"Kindness" spreads like sunshine's glow,
"Sorry" helps when feelings grow.
"Brave" can lift you when you're down,
And "smile" can chase away a frown.

Words can open any door,
They make us dream, they help us soar.
With "please" and "thanks," we show respect,
And with "hope," our lives connect.

But words, my friend, can also sting,
So speak the ones that joy will bring.
Choose them wisely, make them true,
Because your words create the you!

Words are keys to secret lands,
They build great castles in the sands.
With "imagine," they can make you fly,
Or touch the stars up in the sky.

"Explore" can lead to places new,
"Discover" shows the hidden view.
"Encourage" helps a friend feel strong,
"Persist" reminds us to hold on long.

"Adventure" calls to climb and roam,
While "cherish" brings a feeling of home.
"Learn" unlocks the wonders of all,
And "believe" helps us stand tall.

Words are bridges, wide and vast,
They link the future to the past.
So speak with care, and let words shine,
For their magic is yours and mine!

3. Vivekananda: The Youth Icon

In 1893 a beacon born to spread the light,
In Kolkata's embrace, a soul took flight.
Narendra shone, so bright, so true,
A child of courage, wisdom grew.

To Ramakrishna, his master divine,
He gave his heart, his soul, his time.
With love and service, his faith did glow,
A path of truth, he vowed to show.

A youth of vision, bold and wise,
He saw the world through fearless eyes.
Awaken, rise, and lead the way,
The future rests on you today.

In Banaras once, a monkey chase,
He turned around, his fears to face.
Face your troubles, do not flee,
For courage sets the spirit free.

At school, he stood for what was right,
Took the blame with fearless might.
Truth is strength, his life displayed,
On honesty's path, his soul was laid.

With books, his mind became a sea,
Each word retained with clarity.
Focus builds the strongest mind,
Through practice, strength is what you'll find.

Upon the champak tree, he climbed,
Ignoring tales of demons' time.
Fear is false, his heart would sing,
For truth defeats the darkest thing.

In America, with steady hand,
He aimed and showed the crowd his stand.
Focus is power, he taught that day,
Success is born from thoughts that stay.

To a woman who longed for a son,
He gave her love, and blessings won.
Be my mother, he gently said,
Her joy and pride forever spread.

In Khetri's halls, the music played,
He stayed to honor the love conveyed.
Respect the hearts that deeply feel,
In every soul, there lies the real.

At Chicago, he took the stage,
A monk whose words broke every cage.
Brothers, sisters, his message clear,
United all, far and near.

Through every village, town, and street,
He served the poor with hands and feet.
Serve humanity, serve the divine,
In every life, the Infinite shines.

Awake, arise, and stop not till,
Your dreams align with strength of will.
Let courage guide you through the strife,
For fear defeats the joy of life.

Strength is life, and fear is death,
Live with courage, till your last breath.
The brave will always find their way,
While doubt will lead the heart astray.

The soul within is bright, divine,
A spark of truth, a flame that shines.
Know thyself, the highest goal,
Discover the power within your soul.

Unselfish hearts will always endure,
Through love and work, so true and pure.
The climb is hard, the summit steep,
But joy rewards the faith you keep.

Have faith in yourself, the strength inside,
Let courage be your constant guide.
Each step you take, let purpose show,
The power within will help you grow.

Work is worship, a sacred call,
Through selfless acts, you serve us all.
In every task, the Divine is near,
Let love and duty conquer fear.

4. Keeping an Honest Character

In life's vast stage, where shadows play,
An honest soul lights up the way.
Through twists and turns, it firmly stands,
A fortress built by steady hands.

No treasure glows like truth inside,
No power breaks what values guide.
The heart that beats in pure refrain,
Knows no deceit, bears no stain.

Through stormy winds and blazing skies,
An honest path will never lie.
It shapes the soul, it builds the name,
A beacon bright, a steady flame.

The world may tempt with fleeting gold,
Yet virtue stands, unbought, unsold.
Its weight is light, its course is clear,
It walks in faith, devoid of fear.

The mask may fade, the guise may fall,
But truth will stand above it all.
For every lie, a shadow grows,
And with it, peace forever goes.

An honest heart brings endless peace,
Its joy is pure, its strength won't cease.
No fear of doubt, no need to hide,
It walks with grace, a worthy guide.

The path of truth is rarely smooth,
It tests the brave, it sharpens youth.
But those who walk with head held high,
Will find their wings to touch the sky.

Deeds define the tales we leave,
Not wealth amassed, nor webs we weave.
An honest act, a kind embrace,
Outshines the glitter time will erase.

Through every trial, keep this near,
Let truth be armor, calm your fear.
No battle scars, no fleeting fame,
Can tarnish honor's timeless name.

In fleeting moments, life is told,
Not by the riches, nor by gold.
But by the echoes left behind,
Of love, of truth, of hearts aligned.

Each word you speak, each step you take,
A ripple in the world you make.
Let honesty guide every choice,
Its whispers grow to thunderous voice.

No storms can shake a steadfast will,
No lies can match a heart that's still.
The calm of truth, a quiet stream,
Reflects the world as it should seem.

One who stands for what is right,
Will glow with grace, a guiding light.
And shall build a world of love and trust,
A legacy that's fair and just.

Mistakes may come, and trials too,
Yet truth will see you through and through.
For honest hearts, though hurt may burn,
Will find their peace in time's return.

Betrayal fades, but truth will last,
A bond unbroken, unsurpassed.
It nurtures trust, it heals the pain,
And leaves a mark that shall remain.

So carry forth this precious gift,
Through highs and lows, through every rift.
An honest life, a soul sincere,
Will find its place beyond all fear.

No judge or jury can erase,
The power of an honest face.
A character built strong and true,
Will shine in all the good you do.

And when your story's end is near,
Your name will echo, pure and clear.
For life's true wealth is simply this:
An honest heart, eternal bliss.

5. The Bhagwat Geeta's Allusion

In Kurukshetra's divine light, so pure,
Bhagwat Geeta, a scripture to endure.
Spoken by Krishna, the eternal guide,
It unveils truths where wisdom resides.

Centuries back, Dhritarashtra blind but keen,
Heard through Sanjay, the unseen scene.
Barbarik, too, with vision profound,
Saw fate unfold, yet stood unbound.

Hanuman perched upon Arjun's flag high,
Witnessing dharma's battle under the sky.
A listener, too, in silence he stayed,
As Geeta's wisdom through Krishna played.

Hanuman, unseen, yet shaped the course,
His strength and will, the battle's force.
Arjun, the listener, with courage shaken,
Found in Krishna, his doubts forsaken.

Through Morari, the gardener divine,
Five allusions of Geeta now entwine.
Lessons eternal, for seekers' hearts,
Guiding the soul where the journey starts.

The one who renounces desires and gains,
Who harbors no malice, no lingering chains.
Free from attachments, at peace and clear,
The soul resides where the truth draws near.

To surrender fully is not to proclaim,
But to let go of ego, greed, and name.
Like a mother cherishing her late-born child,
True surrender is patient, deep, and mild.

Leave all behind, the ego, the clench,
Like the vast sky that holds no stench.
For the one who lets go, gains it all,
In the void lies the universe's call.

"Love all," Krishna whispers, the divine decree,
See the self in all, and let others see thee.
Live as if all is yours, and die unbound,
In love's embrace, true peace is found.

"I am not this body, this fleeting breath,
Nor bound by hunger, nor touched by death."
The soul eternal, beyond birth and demise,
Dwells in truth, where illusion dies.

Thus, Geeta's wisdom, timeless and true,
Unveils paths for seekers old and new.
With Krishna's voice and a Sadguru's grace,
The soul ascends to its destined place.

6. The Soul Remains

This body wakes, this body sleeps,
Through seven stages, time it keeps.
From infant soft to child at play,
Then love and youth soon pass away.

A judge so wise, with steady mind,
Then years of rest, as fate's designed.
Old age arrives with steps so slow,
Yet soul untouched still shines aglow.

The body bends, its strength is lost,
Like autumn leaves in winter's frost.
But deep within, no time can chain,
The soul untouched will still remain.

No sword can cut, no fire can burn,
No storm can shake, no tides can turn.
It's never born, it does not fade,
Beyond all time, it's ever stayed.

This shell we wear will fall someday,
Like clothes once worn, then cast away.
Yet we are more than flesh and bone,
A light divine, forever known.

Through youth and age, through joy and pain,
Through fleeting loss and fleeting gain,
The body breaks, yet still we be,
A soul beyond mortality.

Unborn, undying, firm and true,
It stays when all is lost from view.
So fear not death, nor passing years,
For what we are will persevere.

This body's made of earth and air,
Of fire, water, space so bare.
With mind and senses, nature's field,
Yet soul alone holds truth revealed.

Desires rise, and sorrows stay,
Joy and grief drift on their way.
Yet like the sky, so vast, so free,
The soul remains—untouched, at peace.

Embrace the path, walk free, walk bold,
This truth is bright, this truth is old.
The body fades, the soul remains,
Unchanged through time, untouched by chains.

7. The Trial at the Lake

In the forest deep and wide,
Where Pandavas chose to hide,
A scorching sun, a day so dry,
Made their thirst and hunger rise.

First went Nakul, young and brave,
To find a pond, his thirst to stave.
He saw the water, clear and bright,
But a voice warned him, full of might:

"Answer me, before you drink,
Or death will come in just a blink."
Ignoring words, he drank in haste,
And fell down still, his life erased.

Then Sahadev was sent to see,
What had happened, where could he be?
Finding Nakul cold and still,
He rushed to drink, against the will.

The same voice spoke, the warning same,
But Sahadev too, lost the game.
His body fell, his breath was gone,
The curse of Yaksha carried on.

Arjun came with bow in hand,
Like a warrior, took his stand.
"Who dares to slay my kin?" he cried,
But the Yaksha's voice replied:

"Not by arrows, not by might,
Only wisdom wins this fight."
Arjun too ignored the call,
Drank the water, doomed to fall.

Mighty Bhima, fierce and strong,
Reached the place, but not for long.
He saw his brothers, lifeless there,
Yet took the sip without a care.

Like the rest, he too was gone,
A silent lake, but full of wrong.
At last came Yudhishthir wise,
With sorrow deep within his eyes.

He saw them lying, pale and dead,
But took no step where danger led.
Then Yaksha spoke, with thunder loud,
"Answer me, make me proud!"

"What is heavier than the land?"
"A mother's love, a touch so grand."
"What is taller than the sky?"
"A father's grace, none can deny."

"What runs faster than the breeze?"
"A restless mind that never sees."
"What outnumbers all the trees?"
"Worries vast as endless seas."

"What is a dying man's true friend?"
"Charity, till the very end."
"What brings peace and joy alike?"
"Compassion pure, burning bright."

"What blinds the world in endless night?"
"Ignorance, that dims the light."
"What is the greatest wonder here?"
"Men see death, yet live with cheer."

Yaksha smiled, his test was won,
The eldest brother, the righteous one.
"A boon I grant, choose one to live,"
"Only one, the chance I give."

Yudhishthir thought, and then he spoke,
"Let Nakul rise, my words invoke."
Yaksha paused, with curious gaze,
"Why not Bhima, why this phrase?"

"Kunti and Madri, mothers both,
Deserve a son to keep their oath.
I still stand, Kunti's kin,
Let Nakul live, let justice win."

Yaksha, pleased, revealed his form,
Dharma stood, so bright and warm.
"You have won, your heart is pure,
Your brothers live, your path is sure."

Thus they rose, with breath anew,
The lake once cursed, a blessing too.
For wisdom, patience, truth so high,
Had saved them all from fate so dry.

8. The Song of the Eternal

(A Poetic Reflection on the 18 Chapters of the
Bhagavad Gita)

1. The Despair of Arjuna (Arjuna Vishada Yoga)

Upon the battlefield, his heart did shake,
A warrior strong, yet his soul would break.
Torn between duty, love, and pain,
In silent sorrow, he wept in vain.

2. The Path of Knowledge (Sankhya Yoga)

"Rise, O Arjuna!" the Lord declared,
"For wisdom shines when souls are bared.
This body fades, the soul remains,
Beyond all losses, beyond all gains."

3. The Yoga of Action (Karma Yoga)

"Act, yet claim not the fruit," He spoke,
"Do your duty—let go the yoke.
For selfless work, in love performed,
Is the fire where bondage is transformed."

4. The Path of Wisdom (Jnana Yoga)

"When wisdom dawns, the night is bright,
Truth alone is the guiding light.
Seek the wise, and learn with grace,
The soul eternal knows no place."

5. The Yoga of Renunciation (Karma Vairagya Yoga)

"Renounce not work but all desire,
Let actions burn in devotion's fire.
A sage in stillness, yet he moves,
For in detachment, peace improves."

6. The Yoga of Meditation (Dhyana Yoga)

"Calm your mind, be still, be free,
Like the windless lake, like the silent sea.
Through breath and thought in union deep,
Find the truth where shadows sleep."

7. The Yoga of Wisdom and Devotion (Jnana Vijnana Yoga)

"Know Me, seeker, beyond the veils,
I am the wind that fills your sails.
Through love and wisdom, come to Me,
As rivers rush to meet the sea."

8. The Imperishable Brahman (Aksara Parabrahma Yoga)

"When time dissolves and night descends,
The soul ascends where life transcends.
Those who seek Me at their last breath,
Shall break the chains of birth and death."

9. The Yoga of Royal Knowledge (Raja Vidya Raja Guhya Yoga)

"A treasure hidden, yet open wide,
A kingly secret none can hide.
Faithful hearts, with love so pure,
Shall find in Me their truth secure."

10. The Yoga of Divine Glories (Vibhuti Yoga)

"In sun and moon, in fire and rain,
In wisdom deep, in battle's strain,
Know My power, in all you see,
For all that shines derives from Me."

11. The Vision of the Cosmic Form (Vishwarupa Darshana Yoga)

The veil was torn, the heavens bright,
A thousand suns in blinding light!
Time devours, creation spins,
Yet love eternal still begins.

12. The Path of Devotion (Bhakti Yoga)

"With love alone, the heart ascends,
No wealth, no power, no mind pretends.
A leaf, a flower, or whispered prayer,
Offered with love, I shall be there."

13. The Field and the Knower (Ksetra Ksetrajna Vibhaga Yoga)

"This body, Arjuna, is but the field,
Where seeds of thought and action yield.
But know the Knower, beyond all claim,
Unmoved, untouched, yet all the same."

14. The Three Gunas (Gunatraya Vibhaga Yoga)

"Light and darkness, passion bright,
Bind the soul in veils of night.
Yet those who rise, who wisdom seek,
Shall cross beyond where fetters leak."

15. The Supreme Self (Purushottama Yoga)

"Like a tree whose roots ascend,
Whose branches to the earth extend,
Cut through illusion, stand upright,
Know the Self, the source of light."

16. The Divine and the Demonic (Daivasura Sampad Vibhaga Yoga)

"Two paths there are—the dark, the light,
One leads to peace, one into night.
Fear and greed shall hearts enslave,
But truth and love shall souls engrave."

17. The Threefold Faith (Sraddhatraya Vibhaga Yoga)

"Faith defines the path you tread,
Of wisdom bright, or passions red.
But selfless hearts, in dharma deep,
Shall sow the peace their souls shall reap."

18. The Liberation through Surrender (Moksha Sannyasa Yoga)

"Give up your fears, give up your claim,
Surrender all, yet be the same.
In Me alone, let burdens cease,
And find within eternal peace."

Epilogue

Thus sang the Lord in wisdom pure,
To guide all hearts, to cleanse, to cure.
Beyond all battles, joy or strife,
His song remains—the song of life.

9. Words Beyond Their Literal Sense

In the garden of speech, where meanings bloom,
Words beyond their literal sense find room.
"Kick the bucket," a phrase so dire,
Yet speaks of life's end, a fleeting fire.

"Burn the midnight oil," to strive till dawn,
With every ounce of effort, we carry on.
"Break the ice," a heart's first sigh,
In moments cold, let warmth apply.

"Hit the nail on the head," so precise,
A truth revealed in one quick slice.
"Throw in the towel," surrender's call,
When battles are lost, yet still, we stand tall.

"A bird in the hand," worth more than gold,
When treasures found are worth more than told.
"Cost an arm and a leg," to pay the price,
For dreams that come at sacrifice.

"Let the cat out of the bag," secrets unfold,
What was hidden is now brave and bold.
"Under the weather," a feeling so mild,
Yet signals a storm, soft yet wild.

"Catch someone red-handed," the thief revealed,
In the act, their fate sealed.
"At the drop of a hat," change takes flight,
A moment's decision, in day or night.

"Go the extra mile," beyond what's asked,
With open heart, unmask the task.
"Spill the beans," the truth comes clean,
In words that break the silence unseen.

"Hit the sack," rest your soul,
Find peace in slumber, make yourself whole.
"Beat around the bush," a gentle dance,
Avoiding truths, a fleeting glance.

"The ball's in your court," make your move,
A moment to decide, to prove or lose.
"Pushing up daisies," a phrase so light,
Yet speaks of death, a quiet flight.

"Cry over spilled milk," let it go,
What's done is done, let past sorrow flow.
"Chase rainbows," a dream so sweet,
Yet in vain, it's hard to meet.

"A leopard can't change its spots," they say,
In the heart, what's true won't fade away.
"Throw caution to the wind," be bold,
Take risks, for new stories are yet to be told.

"Jump on the bandwagon," follow the trend,
In crowds, we seek to blend and bend.
"The tip of the iceberg," much more below,
What we see is just the start, we know.

"A penny for your thoughts," do share,
The wonders of the mind, laid bare.
"The elephant in the room," so tall,
A truth unspoken, felt by all.

"Bite off more than you can chew," too much,
Overburdened hearts, losing touch.
"Call it a day," the work is done,
Rest your spirit, for the race is won.

"Put all your eggs in one basket," so grand,
Yet sometimes, it's hard to understand.
"Throw someone under the bus," betray,
In moments of darkness, they slip away.

"A watched pot never boils," it's true,
Time slows when we expect it to.
"Be in the driver's seat," lead the way,
In control of all that comes your way.

"Cut to the chase," no time to waste,
In simple truths, we find our place.
"In the same boat," we all row,
Through storms and calm, we go.

"Behind the eight ball," in a bind,
Yet the strength to rise, we always find.
"Walk on eggshells," so gentle we tread,
For fear of breaking what's been said.

"Jump the gun," act too fast,
And find that time has slipped past.
"An arm and a leg," to pay the cost,
For everything gained, something is lost.

"Not playing with a full deck," they say,
A puzzle missing pieces, in disarray.
"Burn your bridges," no turning back,
Once the path is gone, there's no track.

"Wear your heart on your sleeve," let it show,
Love and pain in every glow.
"Eat humble pie," admit the fall,
With grace, we rise after all.

"On cloud nine," in bliss we soar,
Beyond the earth, forevermore.
"Steal someone's thunder," take their light,
Yet in the end, it's not our right.

"Miss the boat," a chance gone by,
Yet another awaits, we must try.
"Pay the piper," face the toll,
For every choice, there's a price to hold.

"Cold feet," fear holds you tight,
Before the leap, you lose the fight.
"Under your thumb," control so firm,
Yet freedom calls, a different term.

"Out of the blue," surprise unplanned,
Life's twists come, like grains of sand.
"Break the bank," spend too much,
Yet in wealth, we lose our touch.

"Under the radar," unseen, unknown,
In the shadows, secrets are sown.
"By the book," follow the rules,
But sometimes the heart must be the fool.

"Keep your nose to the grindstone," work all day,
The sweat of labor shows the way.
"Bring home the bacon," feed your soul,
In effort, we find the whole.

"Hit below the belt," a painful strike,
Words that hurt, they never feel right.
"Through thick and thin," we stand together,
Through all storms, no matter the weather.

"Hold your horses," wait and see,
Patience is key, let things be.
"Face the music," accept the sound,
In every note, life's lessons are found.

"Back to square one," start again,
In the game of life, we lose and win.
"On the ball," quick and sharp,
Focused on every beat, every harp.

"Take the bull by the horns," be brave,
In challenges, let courage wave.
"Down to the wire," it's almost done,
When the final moments have begun.

"Get the ball rolling," take the first step,
In every journey, there's a new rep.
"Under the table," hidden from sight,
Secrets whispered in the night.

"Mind your Ps and Qs," act with grace,
In words and deeds, find your place.
"Get cold feet," hesitation grows,
Before the leap, the fear shows.

So here in the garden of meaning deep,
Where metaphors and truths silently creep,
Words beyond their literal sense arise,
Whispering wisdom in poetic skies.

10. Words of Sayings

In the quiet dawn, a bird in hand takes flight,
For two in the bush, the promise isn't quite right.
Actions speak louder, more than words ever could,
What you do in life will define the greater good.

A picture whispers what words cannot say,
An apple a day keeps the doctor at bay.
Better safe than sorry, don't risk the fall,
Prevention is better, than cure for us all.

A rolling stone gathers no moss, it's true,
Don't count your chickens before they hatch, it's due.
Out of sight, out of mind, don't let them stray,
While the early bird catches the worm each day.

A penny saved is a penny earned, they say,
Live and let live, let each one have their way.
If you can't stand the heat, get out of the kitchen,
But know that slow and steady wins, with precision.

Jack of all trades, master of none you see,
What goes around comes around, just wait and see.
Laughter is the best medicine, a healing art,
Where there's smoke, there's fire – truth's start.

The grass is always greener on the other side,
But you reap what you sow, don't run or hide.
What goes up must come down, like the tide,
A fool and his money, they soon will divide.

Don't bite the hand that feeds you, remember that,
You can't have your cake and eat it – that's a fact.
In every cloud, there's a silver lining bright,
Where there's a will, there's always a way to light.

Time is money, don't waste it away,
Don't burn your bridges, just for today.
The best things in life are free, always see,
Cleanliness is next to godliness, let it be.

Too many cooks spoil the broth, they say,
A fool's errand doesn't make the right way.
In life's race, slow and steady wins,
Old habits die hard, the struggle begins.

Every dog has its day, so don't be distressed,
Absence makes the heart grow fonder, truly blessed.
The pen is mightier than the sword we wield,
But silence, at times, is a power concealed.

Rome wasn't built in a day, they know,
Patience is a virtue, let it slowly grow.
When in Rome, do as the Romans do,
You can't change the spots on a leopard, true.

An eye for an eye, makes the world blind,
Where there's love, there's kindness to find.
Don't judge a book by its cover, so dear,
What doesn't kill you makes you stronger, clear.

Make hay while the sun shines, bright,
And make the most of today, before night.
A house divided against itself can't stand,
The truth lies in the silence, it's all planned.

Better late than never, they say,
For what is lost, may come back one day.
You can lead a horse to water, but not make it drink,
You can't teach an old dog new tricks, we think.

Every cloud has a silver lining, unseen,
Life's bittersweet, with moments serene.
The squeaky wheel gets the grease, it's loud,
Two wrongs don't make right, nor make one proud.

Birds of a feather flock together, they fly,
Let bygones be bygones, don't wonder why.
Silence is golden, when words would betray,
A penny for your thoughts, that's what they say.

Familiarity breeds contempt, beware,
But a fool's errand might be beyond compare.
You can't make an omelette without breaking eggs,
But don't bite off more than you can chew, avoid the
dregs.

A leopard cannot change its spots, it's true,
Don't throw the baby out with the bathwater, too.
Let sleeping dogs lie, and don't be rash,
Don't cry over spilled milk, it's just a splash.

What's done is done, don't regret or mourn,
Out of the frying pan, into the fire we're born.
The road less traveled is a path to explore,
Time will tell what we're waiting for.

Two heads are better than one, so wise,
But you can't have your cake and eat it, no lies.
The devil is in the details, look close,
While the early bird finds what it needs most.

A stitch in time saves nine, be wise,
But slow and steady, the race always lies.
An ounce of prevention is better than cure,
In the battle of life, you must endure.

Jack of all trades, yet master of none,
The journey's long, but we're not done.
You can't teach an old dog new tricks, they say,
But in the end, it's love that lights the way.

So here it is, my poetic refrain,
Words of sayings, life's sweetest gain.
Through each proverb, wisdom will stay,
Guiding our hearts, every single day.

11. Pronunciation Hypocrisy of the Words

In English, the twists are endless, you see,
Words that confuse and set the mind free.
From silent letters to sounds so strange,
Here's a journey where pronunciations change.

In the **theatre (thee-uh-tur)**, lights dim and rise,
Down the **aisle (ayl)**, a bouquet **(boo-kay)** held with
pride.
Hidden deep is a **cache (cash)**, so neat,
And in the **chalet (sha-lay)**, we find retreat.

The **colonel (ker-nul)** leads with might,
But around the battlefield lies the **debris (day-bree)** of
the fight.
A small **gnome (nome)** stands in the garden's light,
While the **yacht (yot)** cuts through waters at night.

A golden **vase (vahz)** on the mantelpiece,
By the bustling **quay (key)**, life's gentle release.
The sharp **sword (sord)** can cut through the air,
While the **almond (ah-mund)** whispers of care.

A hidden **niche (neesh)** where secrets lie,
And in its quiet, we face **wrath (rath)** that can't deny.
The warm **scone (skon)** with butter so fine,
Next to the **plaque (plak)** where memories shine.

The fragrant **herb (hurb)** graces the stew,
Along with a **chassis (sha-see)** in a car so new.
The crisp **lettuce (let-is)** on a plate,
In the company of a loyal **clique (cleek)** to create.

The passing **hour (our)** is never still,
Sipped with a **liqueur (lick-er)** in a quiet thrill.
The **isle (ayl)** stands against the wide, open sea,
A **depot (dep-oh)** buzzing, full of energy.

A grand **foyer (foy-ay)** with floors so bright,
Next to a **sachet (sa-shay)** that perfumes the night.
The game of **roulette (roo-let)** spins round and round,
While the **valet (val-ay)** waits without a sound.

The juicy **raspberry (ras-bree)** sweetens the air,
As the **marquis (mar-kwis)** sits without a care.
A smooth **segue (seg-way)** from thought to thought,
In the elegance of **ballet (bal-lay)** we are caught.

The soft **mauve (moave)** shades of the sky,
While the **bruschetta (broo-sket-ah)** is served with a
sigh.
A haunt (**hawnt**) where the whispers roam,
And the lively **café (ka-fay)** feels like home.

A timeless **genre (zhahn-ruh)** of art divine,
In the shimmering waters, the **salmon (sam-un)** shine.
A **courier (koo-ree-er)** with letters in hand,
Delivers a **brooch (broach)** from a far-off land.

The golden **croissant (kwah-son)** starts the day,
While the **epitome (ep-i-tuh-mee)** paves the way.
The **subtle (suh-tl)** art of the spoken word,
Is matched by the **address (uh-dress)** that's heard.

The mischievous **mischief (miss-chiff)** that children
bring,
The gentle **psalm (sahm)** that the choir sings.
A sharp **rapier (ray-pee-er)** duels with grace,
While the silent **corps (core)** marches in place.

A **buoy** (**boy**) bobs in the water's embrace,
Next to a vivid **vignette** (**vin-yet**) in a serene space.
The ripe **apricot** (**ap-ri-kot**) from the tree,
And the delicate **fillet** (**fill-ay**) from the sea.

A perfect **pirouette** (**peer-o-wet**) twirls in the dance,
With the ambitious **entrepreneur** (**on-truh-pruh-nur**)
taking his chance.
A playful **foible** (**foy-buhl**) we all hold dear,
And an elegant **hors d'oeuvre** (**or-derv**) to cheer.

The first **debut** (**day-byoo**) on the stage so bright,
With the sweet **almond** (**ah-mund**) in the soft moonlight.
A creative **vignette** (**vin-yet**) to share with the world,
And the scent of the **aisle** (**ayl**) where flowers are
twirled.

A **bouquet** (**boo-kay**) of memories to keep,
In the pocket of time, we silently sleep.
The quiet **cache** (**cash**) where treasures are stored,
In the **chalet** (**sha-lay**) with room to explore.

The **colonel** (**ker-nul**) commands the fight,
While the **debris** (**day-bree**) scatters out of sight.
The **gnome** (**nome**) stands watch in the yard,
Next to the **yacht** (**yot**) that's never far.

A cherished **vase** (**vahz**) in the gentle breeze,
While we walk on the **quay** (**key**) with such ease.
The sharp **sword** (**sord**) fights with strength,
And the **almond** (**ah-mund**) gives peace at length.

A secluded **niche** (**neesh**) for secrets to lie,
And the furious **wrath** (**rath**) that we can't deny.
The buttery **scone** (**skon**) that we adore,
Next to a **plaque** (**plak**) with memories galore.

The **herb** (**hurb**) adds flavor to our stew,
Alongside a **chassis** (**sha-see**) that's built anew.
The fresh **lettuce** (**let-is**) in the sun,
With a close-knit **clique** (**cleek**) having fun.

The passing **hour** (**our**) takes its toll,
But the rich **liqueur** (**lick-er**) fills the soul.
The **isle** (**ayl**) stands so proud and free,
Next to a **depot** (**dep-oh**) by the sea.

The **foyer** (**foy-ay**) is where we arrive,
With a **sachet** (**sa-shay**) that makes us feel alive.
The wheel of **roulette** (**roo-let**) spins with fate,
While the **valet** (**val-ay**) waits at the gate.

The sweet **raspberry (ras-bree)** on the vine,
While the noble **marquis (mar-kwis)** dines.
A smooth **segue (seg-way)** between our thoughts,
As the dancers perform **ballet (bal-lay)** in their spots.

The shade of **mauve (moave)** is soft on the eyes,
And the delicious **bruschetta (broo-sket-ah)** makes us
rise.
The eerie **haunt (hawnt)** whispers in the night,
While the friendly **café (ka-fay)** fills with light.

The timeless **genre (zhahn-ruh)** of our art,
As the swift **salmon (sam-un)** plays its part.
The **courier (koo-ree-er)** delivers with speed,
While the precious **brooch (broach)** takes the lead.

The flaky **croissant (kwah-son)** so fresh,
And the **epitome (ep-i-tuh-mee)** of success.
The subtle **(suh-tl)** tone of the voice so clear,
As the polished **address (uh-dress)** draws near.

The mischievous **mischief (miss-chiff)** we all indulge,
And the sacred **psalm (sahm)** we all divulge.
The flashing **rapier (ray-pee-er)** in a duel,
While the silent **corps (core)** holds their rule.

The drifting **buoy (boy)** on the endless wave,
While the **vignette (vin-yet)** captures the brave.
The **apricot (ap-ri-kot)** and **fillet (fill-ay)** delight,
As we conclude with a **pirouette (peer-o-wet)** so light.

Through the labyrinth of this poetic spree,
We've uncovered the truths of **hypocrisy (hippo-cri-see)**.
Each word a story, a puzzle, a rhyme,
Shaped by culture, language, and time.

So bow to the words, their rules so sly,
For in their beauty, mysteries lie.
This tapestry woven, a linguistic decree,
Pronunciation (pro-nun-see-ay-shun) hypocrisy of
words, set forever free.

12. Wordplay Wonders

Small as a seed, but **mall** is the place,
Where people gather and dreams interlace.
In the **all** of the crowd, we find our way,
Together we journey, night and day.

Chair beneath me, sturdy and true,
While my **hair** in the wind blows through.
In the **air**, there's a whisper, soft and light,
A message of hope taking flight.

I **this** moment, a breath to behold,
Grasping **his** words, in stories untold.
The truth is **is**, in simple lines,
A life of love where peace shines.

The **heat** of the sun, so strong and bright,
Yet I **eat** my bread, a simple delight.
In the warmth, we gather **at** the dawn,
A new day begins, and the dark is gone.

The **price** of joy is not in gold,
But in **rice** shared, a story told.
Frozen **ice** upon the ground,
But in hearts, warmth will always be found.

A **stone** so firm, a **tone** so clear,
The voice of wisdom we all hold dear.
In **one** moment, we understand,
The power of words, across the land.

A **blink** of an eye, a **link** in time,
A passing thought, so fleeting, sublime.
With **ink**, we write what hearts will say,
To leave a mark that won't decay.

In the **flare** of the night, a spark takes flight,
A whisper of **lare**, guiding through the sight.
The stars **are** alive, with secrets untold,
Their timeless light, both bright and bold.

Plate full of dreams, **late** in the race,
Still, we run, we **ate** at our pace.
Time does not wait, it flows like the sea,
Yet in every moment, we're meant to be free.

Start of a journey, the **tart** of a day,
Where sweet meets sour in every way.
With **art**, we express what words can't say,
A masterpiece born from light's first ray.

A **place** for the soul, where **lace** threads bind,
An **ace** in the hand of the brave and kind.
In the weave of time, both gentle and strong,
We all play our part in the eternal song.

To **steal** a glance, to **teal** the sky,
An endless dream as the days fly by.
With **eal** we swim, in waters so deep,
In the currents of time, we wake from sleep.

To **smile** in the sun, to **mile** the road,
A long journey where stories unfold.
To **lie** beside a world so wide,
And feel the love that will never hide.

To **prick** the truth, to **rick** the hay,
And in the field, we find our way.
With a voice so soft, a shout so **ick**,
We dance together, the world's heartbeat quick.

Plate of hope, **late** but sure,
We **ate** our fill, of dreams so pure.
In the quiet night, we rest, we wait,
For the dawn to bring us something great.

13. The Ripple of Words

In the garden of life, where thoughts bloom vast,
Each word sown, a seed for the future cast.
Tongues are rivers that carve through time,
Building bridges or cliffs that we must climb.

A harsh word is a thorn that pricks the soul,
A melody misplaced, a song unwhole.
But a kind phrase, like sunlight's beam,
Turns winter's frost into summer's dream.

Karma's web, unseen, yet strong,
Binds deeds to fate, where we belong.
Speak with grace, for echoes return,
What fires you spark, you too shall burn.

Two inches of tongue, yet mountains it moves,
Its might no sword or cannon disproves.
A whisper can heal, a scream can tear,
A balance of wisdom demands our care.

Hurt not others with careless flame,
For hearts are mirrors; they reflect the same.
To speak with love, a divine art,
Is the sacred rhythm of a pure heart.

Like a potter shaping clay so fine,
Your words mold lives, like stars align.
Not all storms are heard; silence can sting,
Even quiet can wield a mighty swing.

Choose your tone like an artist's hue,
Paint respect in all that you do.
For life's canvas thrives on gentle shades,
Where dignity blossoms and malice fades.

Speak as a lantern, lighting the way,
And leave behind warmth for another day.
Speak as if eternity hears your sound,
And plant love's seed in the fertile ground.

Let us master words, not be their slave,
For in their echo, our legacy's wave.
So, hold your tongue, let kindness reign,
For hearts once broken, rarely mend again.

14. Woven Words of the Wild

Through forests deep and oceans wide,
Where creatures roam and spirits glide,
A world of wonders, fierce and free,
Unfolds in words for all to see.

A **bale** of turtles drifts so slow,
While a **flock** of birds puts on a show.
A **pride** of lions rules the land,
With strength and might at their command.

A **parliament** of owls so wise,
Observes the world with knowing eyes.
A **murder** of crows in shadows sweep,
Their haunting calls disturb the sleep.

A **gaggle** of geese upon the shore,
Honking tales of days before.
A **raft** of ducks in waters bright,
Gliding smoothly in the light.

A **skulk** of foxes, sly and keen,
Moves unseen through woods serene.
A **troop** of monkeys swings so high,
Chasing dreams across the sky.

A **crash** of rhinos thunders near,
Their mighty steps instill some fear.
A **clan** of meerkats stands alert,
Their tiny forms on golden dirt.

A **mob** of kangaroos takes flight,
Bouncing swiftly out of sight.
A **streak** of tigers on the prowl,
Their striped coats so bold and foul.

A **pack** of wolves beneath the moon,
Howls a lonesome, mystic tune.
A **squadron** of eagles soars with grace,
Carving patterns in sky's embrace.

A **swarm** of bees hums low and deep,
Guarding treasures that they keep.
A **leap** of leopards, fast and free,
Dashes past the jungle tree.

A **huddle** of penguins, side by side,
Braves the cold with frozen pride.
A **paddle** of platypuses plays,
In water's dance on rainy days.

A **mischief** of rats scurries along,
Their tiny feet a hurried song.
A **gambit** of skunks, black and white,
Moves with caution in the night.

A **coalition** of cheetahs race,
Speeding through the open space.
A **lounge** of lizards basks in sun,
Soaking warmth till day is done.

A **wake** of vultures circles high,
Gazing down with piercing eye.
A **bevy** of quails in quiet delight,
Scurries softly out of sight.

A **flurry** of pigeons takes to flight,
Painting patterns, sheer and bright.
A **host** of sparrows sings with cheer,
Their melodies so light and clear.

A **bushel** of canaries yellow,
Sings a tune so sweet and mellow.
A **horde** of hamsters digs so deep,
Through tunnels where their secrets keep.

A **tangle** of snakes in coils tight,
Slithers softly out of sight.
A **trove** of toads on mossy ground,
Croaks their chorus, deep and sound.

A **drift** of swans in waters fair,
Glides with elegance and flair.
A **shiver** of sharks in seas so vast,
Moves in silence, sleek and fast.

A **sundown** of dolphins leaps so high,
Underneath the crimson sky.
A **flotilla** of whales roams the deep,
Where ancient mysteries safely sleep.

A **whisper** of woodpeckers taps,
Echoing through the forest gaps.
A **kettle** of hawks in spirals wide,
Rides the thermals, full of pride.

A **band** of gorillas strong and wise,
Roams the jungle with watchful eyes.
A **trail** of elephants in line,
Marches forth through dust so fine.

A **parade** of peacocks, bright and bold,
Spreads their feathers, tales untold.
A **swoop** of falcons dives with grace,
Racing winds in a deadly chase.

A **zazzle** of zebras, black and white,
Gallops freely in the light.
A **warren** of rabbits underground,
Where little feet make fleeting sound.

A **stand** of flamingos, pink and proud,
Rests beneath a drifting cloud.
A **scoop** of pelicans, beaks so wide,
Sails upon the rolling tide.

From jungle deep to ocean grand,
Through golden plains and desert sand,
Each creature moves in perfect line,
A woven world so wild, divine.

Their names we sing, their tales retold,
In **woven words of the wild**—so bold!
Where nature speaks and echoes stay,
A timeless dance that won't decay.

15. Words That Break Free

In a quiet town, where days stood still,
Lived young Jay with a restless will.
Trapped in routine, dull and gray,
He longed to **break away**.

One evening, fueled by his desire,
He drove off, his heart on fire.
But fate had plans, cruel and stark—
His car **broke down** in the dark.

Frustrated, lost, he felt so small,
As if his dreams would never call.
Tears welled up, hope turned dim,
Till a sudden crash startled him.

A thief had tried to **break in**—
Fear surged, but Jay stayed keen.
With courage firm, his voice rose high,
The thief fled, scared by his cry.

Onward he walked, feet sore and bare,
Till a sage sat beneath branches rare.
The old man spoke, his wisdom deep,
"Your struggles, son, are yours to keep."

"Face them bold, do not dismay,
For strength is built along the way.
To **break out of** your darkest night,
You must endure, then find the light."

His words **broke through** Jay's despair,
A beacon bright in hopeless air.
He vowed to **break up** with doubt,
To silence fears that screamed throughout.

But change was tough, not light nor swift,
Like **breaking in** new boots that lift.
Each step was rough, yet step he took,
Trading fear for courage's book.

He chose to **break off** from those,
Who crushed his dreams, who mocked his goals.
He dared to **break with** old belief,
And sought a path that brought relief.

Through every storm, through highs and lows,
He found a way to **break through** woes.
Years ahead, his tale was told,
A story of a heart so bold.

Now in his town, where he once cried,
He stands with strength, his soul untied.
For Jay had learned—so clear to see,
That one must **break free** to truly be.

16. Words That Bring Change

In Satyapur, where wisdom grows,
Lived Sage Raghunath, who always knows.
With truth and love, he'd **bring about** change,
A path of light, through hearts so strange.

Aarav came, with questions deep,
"How can we **bring about** peace to keep?
How can we **bring along** the light,
In a world so dark, to make it right?"

The sage then smiled and softly spoke,
"I'll **bring forth** a tale to give you hope."

(The Story of Dev and Anaya)

In a faraway land, a prince did stand,
Dev, with truth, his heart so grand.
Anaya, kind, with love to **bring along**,
Together they dreamed where hearts belong.

They saw the world, with sorrow and pain,
And hoped to **bring together** love again.
But when the king's court was filled with fight,
They knew they must **bring up** the light.

They set to work, with hearts so true,
To **bring in** kindness, in all they knew.
They **brought together** the lost and weak,
Spreading hope with every word they'd speak.

A farmer's land was taken by force,
Dev knew he must **bring forward** the course.
He stood before the king, his voice so clear,
But corrupt ministers tried to bring fear.

Yet they **brought out** the truth to show,
A plot of lies that caused the woe.
With courage strong, they **brought to light**,
The truth was clear, the wrongs made right.

But Dev grew ill, and Anaya stayed,
She cared for him, while hope did fade.
She **brought him around** with love so pure,
And soon he healed, his strength secure.

Together again, they took the stand,
They **brought forward** the truth to the land.
The ministers fell, the truth was crowned,
The kingdom's peace was safe and sound.

The king then asked, with heart so kind,
"**Bring in** your wisdom, lead and guide."
They ruled with love, and peace did grow,
A land where kindness always flowed.

(Back to the Present)

Raghunath smiled and spoke once more,
"Now, do you see what we have in store?
Truth and love will always **bring off** change,
A world of kindness, free from pain."

Aarav bowed, with heart now bright,
"I will **bring forth** this truth and light.
Wherever I go, I'll **bring along** peace,
And let love's journey never cease."

With steady steps, he walked ahead,
To **bring over** the world, and help it spread.
For in each act, no matter how small,
He could **bring about** peace to all.

17. Carrying Dreams to Reality

In a village small, where dreams were few,
A woman named Meera had a vision true.
She dreamed of a school to light up the day,
A future for children, a brighter way.

Though doubts surrounded her every step,
She **carried on**, through fear and misstep.
The villagers questioned, "Will it succeed?"
But Meera's heart was firm, her will to lead.

She **carried through**, despite the cries,
Her spirit unbroken, her hopes still high.
With passion fierce, she **carried along**
The few who believed, who sang her song.

Through obstacles thick and troubles wide,
She **carried forward**, no fears to hide.
The stormy rains, the lack of funds,
Yet she **carried out** plans, and rallied the ones.

When warned that dreams could soon be lost,
She refused to let her hopes be tossed.
"**Carry away** despair," she boldly said,
For in her heart, hope was never dead.

She worked with heart, with hands, with might,
To **carry out** the task, to set it right.
Through endless hours, her effort grew,
Every donation made her dream anew.

The rains would flood, the site would stall,
But Meera **carried on**, through it all.
When workers faltered, she **carried them along**,
With strength, with courage, and a steadfast song.

The cracks appeared, the foundation shook,
But Meera didn't give up, she didn't look.
She **carried out** repairs with even more care,
Building a future that was strong and fair.

With each challenge faced, she learned and grew,
Carrying others through times that were blue.
Her dream was not just hers to hold,
It was a story of hope, a tale to be told.

The school stood tall, its doors opened wide,
A symbol of dreams that could not hide.
It **carried off** a sense of pride and cheer,
A place where children's hopes drew near.

Through all the work, she had **carried through**,
A legacy strong, a vision true.
The children walked in with dreams to unfold,
A future bright, with stories bold.

But even then, Meera knew the way,
To **carry on**, to build each day.
For the school was not the end, but a start,
A place to **carry dreams** straight to the heart.

The children would **carry with** them the light,
Of knowledge and dreams, to soar to great heights.
The seeds of change had been carefully sown,
And in their hands, the future would be known.

Through all her struggles, her fight, her pain,
Meera's dream had broken every chain.
The school was built, with love and grace,
And hope was **carried forward** to a better place.

So, when the journey felt too long, too wide,
Meera **carried on**, with the strength of pride.
For she knew that, in the end, the day would come,
When others would **carry on**, and the dream would be
won.

A tale of hope, of dreams, of light,
The school that **carried hope**, so bright.
And as it stands, it still reminds,
That one person's vision can change many minds.

18. The Comeback Story

One day Rahul **came across** a dream,
An old idea with a hopeful gleam.
To build a future, bold and bright,
Ankit **came along** to share the fight.

But troubles struck, things **came apart**,
Failure tried to break his heart.
Yet hope returned and **came around**,
With courage strong, new paths were found.

A rival **came at** them, fierce and loud,
But they stood tall and firm, unbowed.
Through ups and downs, they **came back** strong,
Determined to right what once went wrong.

Funds were scarce, none **came by**,
Prices high and hopes ran dry.
They waited for costs to **come down**,
Yet illness struck and brought them down.

Their health declined, they **came down with** pain,
But help **came forward**, hope rose again.
With wisdom shared, they **came in** stride,
Struggles turned to strength inside.

A fortune lost then **came into** sight,
A blessing small but shining bright.
Yet plans they made did not **come off**,
The road to dreams still rough and tough.

"Rise again! Oh, **come on** strong!"
Ankit cheered, "We've come so long!"
Then fame arrived, their name **came out**,
The world took notice, loud and proud.

New chances **came over**, doors opened wide,
But storms still raged, they had to stride.
Through darkest nights, they **came through**,
Their dreams and hopes, they made them true.

The numbers rose, all **came to** shine,
A brand now built with work divine.
A challenge new then **came up** fast,
To grow abroad and make it last.

They worked and planned, they **came up with** ways,
To light their dreams in golden rays.
Through every fall and **come at** storm,
They fought for dreams and rose reborn.

For when tough times **come around** to stay,
The strong will fight, not run away.
And if you work with heart and grace,
Success will surely **come your way**.

19. Get Ahead Of

In Vidyanagar, a town so bright,
Taught Chirag Sir, a guiding light.
An English lecturer, wise and strong,
Who helped his students all along.

Though challenged, he would never sway,
His spirit soared, come what may.
With wisdom deep and lessons grand,
He shaped young minds with steady hand.

"Get ahead," he'd firmly say,
"Five years of work will pave your way."
"Get on track, don't go astray,"
"A lifetime's joy is not far away."

Yet in the staffroom lurked a foe,
A teacher filled with bitter woe.
With jealousy and words unkind,
He tried to shake Chirag's mind.

He spread false tales, he whispered lies,
He tried to dim Sir's hopeful skies.
But Chirag Sir just stood up tall,
He wouldn't let his spirit fall.

"Get through this," he told himself,
"My work speaks louder than their stealth."
Students watched and soon they knew,
The truth in all that Sir would do.

Aarav, Neha, bright and keen,
Worked with focus, stayed serene.
"Get rid of" doubts, they heard him say,
And climbed the steps to a brighter day.

"Get down to" work, he'd always advise,
"No room for excuses, be focused and wise!"
With every lesson, with every word,
His students' dreams began to be heard.

But Rohan, lost in lazy thought,
A shortcut to success he sought.
He thought he'd just **get by** somehow,
But found regret was waiting now.

Instead of books, he'd **get into** fun,
Thinking his studies could be outrun.
But time went by, and soon he knew,
That success comes to just a few.

He found himself **get stuck** in fear,
His wasted time was now so clear.
The path was lost, the race was gone,
And all his dreams were left withdrawn.

Years flew past, he felt the pain,
Wishing he could try again.
"Get back on track," he told his mind,
"Hard work alone will help me find."

Through it all, Sir stood so strong,
Teaching right, correcting wrong.
Though doubted by a jealous peer,
His students held his wisdom dear.

"Get serious now," his message clear,
"Your future will shine bright, my dear."
With faith, with grit, they made their way,
Living his words to this very day.

Those who worked, they **got ahead** of peers,
Success and joy replaced their fears.
While those who slacked, they learned too late,
That time once lost won't compensate.

His life was more than just a class,
A guiding force none could surpass.
A lesson lived, a tale well-spun,
A race well-run—Chirag Sir had won!

20. Put to the Test

Aryan dreamed both bold and bright,
But feared to **put across** his vision right.
A contest came, his chance was near,
He chose to **put forward** ideas clear.

He **put aside** his joys and play,
Worked through nights, no time to stray.
His games and fun were **put away**,
For dreams, he'd fight both night and day.

With passion strong, he **put in** might,
Coding till the morning light.
But fate was cruel—his screen went black,
His files were gone, no turning back.

His hopes were crushed, he felt **put down**,
His dream seemed lost, his smile a frown.
Yet deep inside, his fire stayed,
He'd **put together** what had decayed.

With weary eyes, he **put on** drive,
To make his vision stay alive.
No time to waste, he'd **put off** rest,
To prove his work was still the best.

Then came the day, but fate had more,
A call—his father, weak and sore.
It **put him in** a dreadful test,
His heart in turmoil, mind distressed.

His dreams? His dad? A choice so tough,
He chose his love—that was enough.
He **put back** thoughts of self and gain,
And ran to ease his father's pain.

Yet fate was kind, his dad stood strong,
His boss had seen his heart belong.
A chance was given, he'd **put through**,
His pitch with passion, bold and true.

He spoke with fire, no doubts, no fear,
And made sure to **put over** clear.
The judges heard, his dreams took flight,
His vision strong, his future bright.

His project soared, the world stood up,
The company chose to **put up**.
Though life had **put him upon** trials wide,
He faced them all with fearless stride.

Through sweat and tears, he gave his best,
And stood apart from all the rest.
For when you're **put to the test** so deep,
The heights you reach are yours to keep.

21. Turning the World Around

In a town divided, cold and apart,
No love, no trust, no open heart.
Till one fine day, a traveler came,
Rohan, the wise, with hope aflame.

He **turned up** where the town hall stood,
And saw no bonds, no brotherhood.
He **turned to** the mayor, so firm and proud,
"Let's build a bond, unite the crowd!"

But she **turned down** his hopeful plea,
"This town won't change, just let it be."
Yet Rohan knew, change starts small,
And love could **turn around** them all.

He met the youth with open mind,
And showed them how to be more kind.
They took the task and shared his dream,
To **turn back** hate, to build a team.

They needed land, they needed space,
So to Mr. Carson, they pled their case.
At first, he coldly **turned away**,
But kindness made him see the way.

With open heart, he **turned over** ground,
Where love and laughter would be found.
The festival now had its place,
Yet music lacked its healing grace.

A singer known for voice so bright,
Had **turned against** the mayor's light.
But past was past, she let it go,
And let her melodies freely flow.

The children danced but lost their pace,
Yet none **turned on** them in disgrace.
Instead, the wiser lent their hand,
To teach, to guide, to help them stand.

The baker smiled and **turned on** fire,
To feed the poor, to inspire.
The doctor too, his greed cast down,
He **turned down** wealth, to heal the town.

The festival bloomed, a sight so grand,
For all to see, to understand.
That when we share, when we embrace,
The world becomes a kinder place.

And as they cheered, as love grew strong,
Mr. Carson knew he'd been wrong.
So he **turned in** a gift so true,
A center built for all to use.

The town had **turned around** at last,
Their walls of hate, a thing of past.
When storm winds blew, they stood as one,
No fear remained—division, none.

Then Rohan smiled, his work was through,
He'd planted hope, and watched it grew.
He packed his bags, he'd **turned back**,
To spread more love along his track.

"The world's one home," he said so proud,
"One beating heart, one sacred crowd."
"When we unite, when we stand tall,"
"We rise together, we never fall."

Moral:

To **turn against** or **turn away**,
Will keep the world in shades of grey.
But if we **turn to** love, not fear,
A world of peace will soon be near.